D1467334

Starr Presbyterian Church
1717 W. Thirtoen Mile Road
Royal Oak, Michigan 48073

A3139

Presented to

_____

by

_____

_____

_____

_____ , 19 _____

Copyright © 1988
by Brownlow Publishing Company,
6309 Airport Freeway,
Fort Worth, TX 76117

All rights reserved. The use or reprinting
of any part of this book without the express
written permission of the publisher is
prohibited.

Every effort has been made to contact the
various authors of writings in this book;
however, some may not have been located
and are unknown to the writer and publisher.
Questions in this regard should be directed
to the publisher.

All writing in this book not otherwise
attributed is by the author.

Photo on page 63, Comstock

Printed in the United States of America.

ISBN 0-915720-72-8

10 9 8 7 6 5 4 3 2 1

A Few HALLELUJAHS for Your Ho-Hums

Written & Compiled by
MARY HOLLINGSWORTH

Foreword by
FLORENCE LITTAUER

Starr Presbyterian Church
1717 W. Thirteen Mile Road
Royal Oak, Michigan 48073

Brownlow

Brownlow Publishing Company, Inc.

Other Brownlow Gift Books

Dedication

To my dad,
Clyde Shrode,
who loves God,
loves life
and
loves people—
he's one of the best
hallelujahs in
my life.

Foreword

So much of life is boring.
So many books are dull.
So much that is light hearted is trivial.
So much that is deep is confusing.

What a delight it is to pick up a book of hallelujahs that is not ho hum, to enjoy exciting stories that have purpose and to read intelligent phrases that have heart, clarity and spiritual value.

Laugh, love and be lifted up!

With joy and hallelujahs.

Florence Littauer
Founder of CLASS Speakers

A Few Hallelujahs for Your Ho Hums

Life can be a real yawner, a regular ho-hum experience, if you let it. It's a rutted routine of everyday repetition, unless you kick out of the traces and run free.

And yet, the Great Creator is not a ho-hum god. He's the hallelujah God! And we are created in his image to be hallelujah people. He didn't breathe into us the breath of ho-hum existence; he breathed into us the breath of life! He filled us with his Spirit of exhilaration, anticipation and triumph. He inflated us with himself, the very Being of creativity, energy and electricity for living.

God's hallelujah nature is evident wherever you look, if you look with hope. The brilliant variety of flowers, the vibrant colors of landscapes, the antics of his creatures and the delightful rainbow of talents he gives his people all shout "Hallelujah!" The wonders of his world, and beyond, destroy any possibility of a ho-hum existence for those who allow his Spirit to lead them. And those same wonders ignite in us a flame of hope, of happiness and awe.

So, when life becomes ordinary, when you're a little blue or bored with the day-to-day doldrums, just look around you, and perhaps you'll find a few hallelujahs for your ho hums.

Open my eyes that I may see
wonderful things ...
I am a stranger on earth.

—PSALM 119:18-19

Into all our lives, in many simple,
familiar, homely ways, God infuses this element
of joy from the surprises of life, which unexpect-
edly brighten our days, and fill our eyes with
light. He drops this added sweetness into his
children's cup, and makes it to run over. The
success we are not counting on, the blessing we
were not trying after, the strain of music in the
midst of drudgery, the beautiful morning picture
or sunset glory thrown in as we pass to or from
our daily business, the unsought word of
encouragement or expression of sympathy, the
sentence that meant for us more than a writer
or speaker thought—these and a hundred
others that everyone's experience can supply are
instances of what I mean.

—SAMUEL LONGFELLOW

The people were saying:
"Hallelujah!
Our Lord God rules. He is the
All-Powerful.
Let us rejoice and be happy
and give God glory!"

—Revelation 19:6-7
(The Everyday Bible)

The Whitman Sampler

Chocolate! If you don't mind my saying so, the Lord "done good" when he made chocolate. Of course, I contend that if he'd made chocolate taste like celery and celery taste like chocolate we'd all be a lot thinner.

Instead, he made *life* a Whitman Sampler. It's a whole box crammed full of goodies, sweet and gooey with surprise centers. When you're born, God opens up the box of life and says, "Here, have some." And the wonderful thing about it is, life's not even fattening. Eureka!

God's not finicky about the particular flavor of life you choose either. That's why there are different kinds of occupations, hobbies and ministries from which to choose. He doesn't care if you take your finger and punch a hole in the

bottom of a piece of life to see if you like
it and, then if you don't, just put it back in the
box and try something else more to your liking.
He knows that some of us prefer caramel filling
to coconut. And it's okay.

Now, I'm a caramel-and-peanuts fan myself, and that's the kind of life I choose, too. Sometimes it's sweet, sometimes it's chewy, sometimes it's crunchy and salty. Variety is what I like. Sometimes I just like to hold a bit of life in my mouth and let the chocolate melt off until I get to the gooey center. Sometimes I can't wait that long so I just chew it up and let it stick to my teeth.

You can choose your own flavor of life. All you have to do is remove the cellophane wrapper, open life's lid, take out the little paper liner and dig in! And I'll bet God will be grinning from ear to ear because he wanted life to be a delicious experience.

Not Worth the Worry

My first paid writing job was on the personal staff of oil billionaire Haroldson Lafayette Hunt, better known as H. L. Hunt and often called "the richest man in the world." Naturally, his being incredibly rich brought the press around on a regular basis.

It was during one of those probing interviews where reporters tried to make a brilliant man into a bumbling fool that Mr. Hunt, as usual, turned the tables. He sat at his desk with a piece of paper in his left hand, his wispy white hair mussed from running his right hand through it, waving the paper to emphasize his answers to their questions.

One reporter baited Mr. Hunt about his sporty son, Lamar, who had bought the Dallas Texan football team and turned them into the Kansas City Chiefs. He said, "Mr. Hunt, Lamar has lost over a million dollars a year on a football team. Doesn't that worry you?"

Mr. Hunt paused for a moment, as

if mentally calculating, and then said,
"Well, the way I figure it, if Lamar lost a
million dollars a year, he'd be broke in about
450 years." Then he grinned his "gotcha" grin,
and his blue eyes twinkled with delight, as I'd
seen them do so often.

Relatively speaking, many trivial things
in life are just not worth the worry. Worry is
the clutter of life. It clutters your thinking,
clutters your emotions and makes you
ineffective. It takes the hallelujah out of life.
It's far better to put those worry warts in
perspective with the magnitude of life and the
vastness of eternity and just get on with living.
Like Lamar, you don't need to worry about a
few minor losses along the way, because your
Father is incredibly rich. In fact, he owns the
whole world.

Optimism

O ptimism is a five-year-old boy. It's being certain that this time your balloon will not pop or float away. It's being more excited about learning to ice skate than fearing you'll fall down. It's swinging with all your might, even when you already have two strikes and three balls. Optimism is believing an empty gift box is just a clue that the present was too big for the box. And it's blowing the biggest bubblegum bubble in school, knowing that it might pop all over your face at any moment. Optimism is knowing that everything will come out all right, even when it starts out all wrong. It's expecting the best...in people, in life and yourself. It's the hallelujah side of life.

*The pessimist sees the difficulty
in every opportunity; the optimist,
the opportunity in every difficulty.*

—L. P. JACKS

Instead of weeping when a tragedy
occurs in a songbird's life, it sings
away its grief. I believe we could well
follow the pattern of our feathered
friends.

—ROBERT S. WALKER

Inspiration

Some say the inspiration of God is over. He wrote one Book and quit. I doubt it. I don't...I can't...accept creative passivity on the part of The Creator. And every writer knows that writing books is like eating potato chips—you can't stop with just one. Oh, he's still creating all right, and he can do it through me if he wants to, I suppose.

Would I go so far as to say that *I* am an inspired writer? Yessiree. Sounds pretty arrogant, doesn't it? Truthfully, it makes me a little nervous to think about it, too, but here's how I figure it. The word *inspired* means "God breathed," and the Bible says that "God breathed into man the breath of life." He *inspired* mankind from the very beginning. He breathed his own creative spirit into us. So, I must be inspired.

Oh, I know that my writing is not *the* word of God, but I pray that he uses me as his writing instrument to communicate thoughts about him to the world. I certainly can't take credit for what I write. Ideas seem to come out of nowhere at times. I wake up in the night with something on my mind that must be written down. I hear music that stimulates hopes and dreams and wonder that must be shared.

Now, perhaps, you wouldn't call that inspiration. That's okay, but I prefer to believe that God works through me, that God lives in me, that God shares himself with you through me and words he writes through me, just as he shares himself with me through you and your gift of encouragement, music or art. After all, if God could speak eloquently through a critter like Balaam's donkey, surely...surely, he can say *something* worthwhile through me and my stubby pencil. Just think what he'll be able to do when I get a computer with a heavenly hook-up!

There are one-story intellects, two-story intellects, and three-story intellects with skylights. All fact collectors, who have no aim beyond their facts, are one-story men. Two-story men compare, reason, generalize, using the labors of fact collectors as well as their own. Three-story men idealize, imagine, predict; their best illumination comes from above, through the skylight.

—OLIVER WENDELL HOLMES

Every person has a gift for communicating in a unique and personal way. It is God's gift to you. Your gift to God is to discover the talent he has hidden in you and use it to proclaim his glory to the world around you. Let your poem or picture or song cause the world around you to say, "Hallelujah!"

I cannot write poetically, for I am no poet.
I cannot artfully arrange my phrases
    so as to give light and shade.
Neither am I a painter;
Nor can I even express my thoughts by
    gesture and pantomime,
    for I am no dancer.
But I can do so in sounds. I am a musician.

—WOLFGANG AMADEUS MOZART

Moving On

When I was a kid, we moved around a lot. At last count, my mom and dad had moved forty-seven times. In fact, my mom once commented that if the TV ever got unplugged, it wrapped its cord around itself and ran out on the front porch to wait for the moving van. She laughingly claimed that she could blow a whistle and our furniture would pile itself up in the corner.

Oh, go ahead and laugh, but there was one house in Greenville, Texas, that we moved in and out of three different times! And, Greenville, not being a metropolis, only had two moving companies; so, we had the same two men from Frank Wolfe Movers for all three moves—George and Leroy. I can remember their names because they sounded like a vaudeville team.

The third time they came to move us out of the house on Caddo Street was like old home week. Those guys were practically part of the family by then. George asked about Rags, our dog, and Leroy wanted to know when we had bought the upright piano that wasn't there the last time they had moved us.

One thing was different that time though. Harry also came from Wolfe to help with the move. You can imagine his surprise at the welcome home they received. Finally, tired of the unproductive conversation, he said, "George, we might as well start with this couch first."

George said, "No, Harry, you've got to go back there in the back bedroom and get that round oak table; it fits right up in the front corner of the truck."

Everybody laughed but Harry. Nonetheless, they loaded the round oak table first. And when we arrived at the new house, George and Leroy placed almost all the furniture in the right rooms with virtually no help from us. It was one of the easiest moves we ever made.

Well, we should always be moving on, moving from the ho hum toward the hallelujah, especially in our spiritual lives. If we do it often enough and get lots of practice, moving into our heavenly home will be the easiest move we ever make, especially if we use the same Moving Man every time.

Ah, but a man's reach should exceed his grasp, or what's a heaven for?

—ROBERT BROWNING

I.D.T.A.

Opera star Beverly Sills wears a piece of jewelry with the initials "I.D.T.A." engraved on it. When a friend expressed concern that Beverly was going to stop singing to become director of the New York City Opera in 1979, she pointed to the initials, which stand for "I Did That Already."

Having sung for so long, she felt it was time to move on. She didn't want to repeat, again and again, what she has mastered. She felt a new sense of purpose in moving on to unexplored terrain. Why not break out of *your* routine? Say, "I Did That Already," and move on.

*There is nothing noble in being
superior to some other men; the
true nobility is in being superior
to your previous self.*

—HINDU PROVERB

Perhaps it is a good thing that you
haven't seen all your dreams come true. For
when you get all you wish for, you will be
miserable. Alexander the Great conquered
the world, but he died of sheer boredom. To be
forever reaching out, to remain unsatisfied, is
the key to spiritual progress.

—N. C. CHRISTIAN ADVOCATE

The Real Dream

When you wake up in the morning and remember mental scenes that skipped through your sleep, you say, "I must have been dreaming." Sometimes those scenes are adventures in vivid technicolor; other times they are only snatches of events or a familiar face in black and white.

Now, my perspective is quite different, because when I lie down at night ready to turn out the lamp of my mind, I reflect over the day and think, "I must have been dreaming."

What else could life be but a dream? You arise to a glorious sunrise in the east, painted by the airbrush of heaven. You're greeting by family or friends, whose smiling faces say, "I love you just as you are." You breathe fresh air that exhilarates and sustains you from dawn to dawn. You face challenges to your intelligence, creativity, skills and personality in a job that offers a fair wage or a personal satisfaction. And you come home to a comfortable chair, entertainment piped right into your living room, good food, an electric blanket, a soft pillow for your head and a pet that loves you, no matter what.

So I ask you, if that's not a dream, what is it? Life is the dream! Chase it, and you'll chase away your ho hums.

I consider that our present sufferings are not worth comparing with the glory that will be revealed in us.
—ROMANS 8:18

Or, to put it another way, I consider that our present ho hums are not worth comparing to the hallelujahs that will be revealed in us.

To Lament or Laugh

When my friend Charlotte moved into her new house, we spent several hours unpacking boxes and finally worked our way into the kitchen. She wanted to wash all the dishes before putting them away; so, we unpacked a couple of boxes and loaded the dishes into the dishwasher, only to discover that we couldn't find the automatic dishwashing detergent.

I said, "That's no problem; we'll just use this dishwashing liquid."

"Are you sure?" she said. "I thought you couldn't use regular liquid detergent in a dishwasher."

"Oh, not really," I said. "I've done it before, and it worked fine."

So, I filled up both detergent cups on the dishwasher door, closed the door and turned on the dishwasher. Then, we went back into the dining room to continue unpacking.

About ten minutes later, I walked past the kitchen door and glanced in. The entire kitchen floor was covered with soap suds, and they were getting deeper by the

second. But I didn't panic.

I said, "You know, Char, you were right. You *can't* use liquid detergent in a dishwasher after all." *She* panicked!

The next hour was like a rerun of an "I Love Lucy" show. Every time I pushed the sponge mop into the soap suds, the whole sudsy floor moved away from me like a glacier. Charlotte finally held a wide-mouthed pan to the floor, and I chased the suds into the pan with the mop. She would pour them into the sink, rinse them down and we'd start again.

We were winning the battle until we ventured to open the dishwasher door to face a solid wall of soap suds. We quickly slammed the door shut, trapping most of the suds inside. We decided the thing to do was to put the dish-washer on "Rinse" to wash away the suds.

Wrong! The hot water just multiplied the soap suds and sent them bubbling onto the kitchen floor again. And we were back to square one. Finally, using the sprayer hose on the sink, we were able to dissolve the suds with cold water. By then we were so tired from mopping and laughing we just went to bed. We decided that it was not the ideal method to employ but that she did, in fact, have the cleanest kitchen floor we'd ever seen.

It was one of those hallelujah serendipities that comes from a seeming disaster. It usually has to do with your attitude. You can lament or laugh. You can groan or giggle. You can snarl or smile. It's your choice. Either way, you end up with a clean floor—the serendipity—and that should be good for a small lip twitch or two.

It better befits a man
to laugh at life
than to lament over it.

—SENECA

God's Little Workshop

T here was a small sign over the door that read "God's Little Workshop." It was the laboratory of Dr. George Washington Carver, and he proved its truth throughout his brilliant life.

The story goes that Dr. Carver once held a simple peanut in his hand and asked God to tell him its secret. Then, as if God had actually spoken to him, Dr. Carver suddenly remembered the three scientific laws that had already come from God—the principles of temperature, pressure and compatibility.

At that point, and trusting God's lead, Dr. Carver began uncovering the incredible wealth of the tiny peanut. He discovered such properties as proteins, oils, cellulose, pigments and carbohydrates. Then, putting these properties to work, he created over three hundred products from the peanut, including dyes, stains, soaps, rubber, beverages, shoe polish, milk, leathers and explosives.

God took a slave boy, who had once been swapped for a racehorse, and led him to be one of the world's greatest scientists. He was able to do it because God's great servant believed that his laboratory was God's little workshop, not his own.

So, the next time you feel as if you're only "working for peanuts," think of Dr. Carver and the vast wealth he discovered in one of God's tiny creations. Then consider turning your ho-hum life into God's little workshop, and watch the hallelujahs emerge.

Creative Imagination

I t was in West Africa in 1927 that a blood specimen was taken from a black native named Asibi who was sick with yellow fever. This specimen was inoculated into a rhesus monkey which had just been received from India. Asibi recovered, but the monkey died of the disease. All the vaccine manufactured since 1927, both by the Rockefeller Foundation and other agencies as well, derives from the original strain of virus obtained from this humble native. Carried down to the present day from one laboratory and by enormous multiplication, it has offered immunity to yellow fever to millions of people in many countries. Through the creative imagination of science, the blood of one man in West Africa has been made to serve the whole human race.

—Rockefeller Foundation Report

It was Jerusalem in A.D. 33 when the blood of another man was spilled, and the blood of that simple carpenter has been

available to save the whole human race. And, yet, it was not through the creative imagination of science, but it was through the ultimate plan of The Creator himself. Carried down to the present day from one Christian to another and by remarkable multiplication, it offers immunity to death from the disease of sin to all people in every country. Hallelujah!

Even Exchange

The most agreeable of all companions is a simple, frank man, without any high pretensions to an oppressive greatness; one who loves life, and understands the use of it; obliging, alike at all hours; above all, of a golden temper, and steadfast as an anchor. For such an one we gladly exchange the great genius, the most brilliant wit, the profoundest thinker.

—GOTTHOLD EPHRAIM LESSING

There is no power on earth that can neutralize the influence of a high, pure, simple and useful life.

—BOOKER T. WASHINGTON

Logic

Kim was only three years old. Her sisters, Ronda and Julie, were about five and seven. When it came time to help the mother cow give birth, they wanted to watch. And, life being lived "in the raw" on the farm, their mama saw no reason why they shouldn't see it now as later.

It was a long, difficult ordeal. After forty-seven minutes of huffing and puffing, the little white-faced calf was finally born. The girls' dad and granddad, not to mention the cow, were exhausted. The two men leaned up against the barn wall to catch their breath and wipe the sweat out of their faces. It was at that precise moment that little Kim, peering between the rails of the stall, chose to pose a three-year-old's logical question.

"Well, Dad," she said, "how'd that thing get in there anyway?"

Now, if you think Dad was out of breath before, that innocent question really caused him to suck air.

The fact is, little Kim just wanted what the rest of us want. She wanted to understand the logic of life. The problem is, life's not always logical. And the wisdom of God cannot always be grasped by the mind of man. Somewhere along in life we have to give up the struggle of trying to understand every detail of God's mind, be content to trust his superior wisdom and relax in his grace. Only then will life really become logical and make sense.

Open Minded

Sam didn't really *intend* to be a trouble-maker; it just sort of turned out that way. The truth is, he was so bright that most teachers couldn't stay ahead of him; so, his active mind looked around for something to occupy itself, and he often ended up in mischief.

On one of those occasions, two frustrated teachers brought Sam by the ear in search of the supervisor, who was also frustrated. The supervisor thought it the better part of wisdom to ask Louis, a weight lifter and fellow teacher, to discuss the problem with Sam.

The supervisor could hear the rather rambunctious discussion, and soon Sam emerged rubbing his painful sitting down place and returned to his classroom much more subdued than earlier. Louis followed him out of the "conference room," which doubled as the janitor's workroom.

"Louis, how'd it go with Sam?" asked the supervisor.

"Oh, he's much more open minded about the situation now," said Louis. "I opened it from the other end."

You've probably heard of referred pain. That's when you stub your toe and your eyes leak in response. What Sam experienced was referred logic, and that happens to a lot of us. Something drastic and painful has to happen in our lives before we become more open minded. I think the Good Lord may cure us of spiritual maladies with a little heavenly acupuncture. He needles us a little in one ho-hum spot of our lives so that we take a dose of hallelujah forgiveness and grace about some pet peeve or personal prejudice. No wonder he's called the Great Physician.

And, like Sam, sometimes we just need to be a little more open minded about things. We can count on God to help us, too, even if he has to open it up from the other end.

Little Things

Some folks think that thrills and excitement come from expensive experiences and shocking surprises. And I couldn't agree less. Oh, I admit that I'm probably silly and sentimental...and gettin' more that way all the time...but my thrills come from the little things in life.

These little things are the serendipities that make rainbows of routine. You open the everyday mail, and there's a sweet letter from a long-time-no-see friend. The doorbell rings, and there stands the tiny boy from next door with a grubby hand full of weeds and daisies he's picked just for you...out of your flowerbed. Your sweetheart calls in the middle of the day just to say, "I love you, and I can't wait to see you." You buy a new outfit, and everybody notices how much weight you've lost. You empty your pockets to do the laundry and discover a dollar you'd stuffed in there the last time you wore that old shirt.

I guess you can just keep your bigtop thrills and hair-raisers. I'll take life's little things...or, maybe they're not so little when you really think of it.

Who's Doing This

H e was only five years old, but he had a big, booming voice with which he would, no doubt, become a preacher, or so his mother thought. He was the little hallelujah in her otherwise ho-hum world.

He was to be the ring bearer in the wedding, including tux, tails and satin pillow. It was a dubious honor in his opinion, but since he had to do it, he was totally in control of the situation. Rehearsal went well, except that his mother thought he was walking a bit too fast down the aisle.

Trying to think ahead and ensure that the wedding went off without a hitch, his mother positioned herself about halfway down the bridal path on the seat next to the aisle.

As expected, when the procession started, his mother decided that Junior was moving too fast. So, just as he got to her

pew, she put her hand out and whispered,
"Slow down, sweetheart."

Junior, insulted by the insinuation,
stopped mid-aisle, laid the satin pillow on the
floor, backed off from his mother, put his hands
on his hips and boomed, "Look here, woman!
Who's doing this—me or you?"

The audience rippled with almost
uncontrolled giggles, his mother slid down into
her pew, and Junior calmly picked up his pillow,
straightened his tux jacket and marched to the
front of the church.

Sometimes when we see other people conducting their lives in a manner different from ours, we feel compelled to try and slow them down or straighten them out. The truth is, they probably have their lives well under control, even if it looks out of kilter to us. Somewhere along life's path we've got to learn to live and let live. We've got to quit trying to control the whole world by making their square pegs fit into our round, philosophical holes. We can't do it anyway; so, why try?

The sooner we learn to spend our time working on our own idiosyncrasies and letting others govern their own lives, the sooner life will relax into pleasantness and peace. Ultimately, God is in control of us all. He will decide what's normal and what's out of control.

Hallelujah! Finally, something that's not my job.

Shalom.

Faith

Faith is a prism, refracting the cheerful light of God into vibrant colors and scattering them into the mundane corners of life.

Without faith, we are as stained glass windows in the dark.

—UNKNOWN

Celebrate Together

J ack became a Christian on Sunday. On Wednesday afternoon his wife Carol gave birth to a beautiful baby girl. Jack, a big, burly guy who had a gruff voice and a flamboyant manner, was thrilled. And he wanted to tell somebody.

The church met on Wednesday evening for Bible study. So, being excited about his new daughter and his new church family at the same time, naturally Jack thought we would all want to hear the good news.

There was a side entrance to the auditorium where the adult class met. When you came in that door, you were standing in front of the audience for all to see. Ron, the local minister, had just stood up to begin the Bible study when Jack burst in the side door beaming and announced for all the world to hear, "It's a girl!"

There were a few muffled giggles, but everyone basically reacted happily. Then Jack bounced past Ron and politely hoisted himself up to sit on top of the communion table, bringing gasps from the conservative group in the rear of the auditorium. Jack was oblivious to anything beyond his exuberance and proceeded to give us a blow-by-blow account of the day's events. Meanwhile, Ron, a highly dignified white-shirt-navy-suit kind of minister, was quickly turning ashen, not quite knowing how to stop Jack politely.

To top off his big announcement, Jack hopped down off the "holy" table and bounded up and down the aisles, handing out cigars to all the men and candy to all the ladies. The first cigar went to Ron whose face instantly flushed from ash to scarlet. And the gasps from the back erupted and then lapsed into shocked silence. I collapsed in laughter on the second pew.

Then, as suddenly as he had burst into the room, Jack was gone—back to the hospital to be with Carol and Super Baby. He didn't even stay for Bible study.

When the guffaws and gasps died down, I glanced up to see Ron still standing in front of the class with his Bible in one hand and the cigar in the other. His feet were frozen in place, and he couldn't, for the life of him, figure out what to say. Finally, with obvious fluster and fumbling, he stuck the cigar in his inside coat pocket and said, "I'll just put this away so no one will smoke it."

At that point I couldn't control myself any longer; so, I escaped to the ladies' room where I went into hysterics. I'm sure the Good Lord was laughing too.

Here's the point: hallelujah happenings shouldn't receive ho-hum responses. Let's learn to celebrate together! Let's rejoice with those that rejoice and not get so stuffed into our shirts of religiosity that the buttons pop off in protest. Way to go, Jack. Thanks for loosening our spiritual ties a bit.

Enthusiasm

Make sure your life is a rare entertainment; it doesn't take anything drastic. You don't have to be gorgeous, wealthy or smart— just very enthusiastic!

—BETTE MIDLAR

Life is action and passion.
It is expected of a man that he
share in the action and passion
of his time under penalty of being
judged not to have lived.

—OLIVER WENDELL HOLMES, JR.

*Wondrous is the strength
of cheerfulness, and its
power of endurance.
The cheerful man will
do more in the same time,
will do it better, will
persevere in it longer,
than the sad or sullen.*

—THOMAS CARLYLE

Hug Away Your Ho Hums

Hugging is healthy. It helps the body's immune system. It keeps you healthier. It cures depression. It reduces stress. It induces sleep. It's invigorating. It's rejuvenating. It has no unpleasant side effects, and hugging is nothing less than a miracle drug.

Hugging is all natural; it is organic, no preservatives, no artificial ingredients and 100 percent wholesome.

Hugging is practically perfect. There are no movable parts, no batteries to wear out, no periodic checkups, no monthly payments, no insurance requirements, theft-proof, non-taxable, non-polluting and, of course, fully returnable.

—FROM A *DEAR ABBY* COLUMN

Hugs will definitely put a few hallelujahs in your ho hums.

Mouse Philosophy

t was Gardner Hall, 1970. I was a senior at the small West Texas college and the designated dormitory assistant or "checker" on my floor. One of the students on my wing was Pam Estes, a good friend. We had lived on the same floor all four years of our college life and often shared the same clothes and room.

Now, Pam was no ordinary lady. She was a favorite on campus—president of this, chairman of that, editor of the college newspaper and many other honors. But Pam, with all her strengths, was terrified of mice. And Gardner Hall in those days had its fair share of the little whiskered rascals.

In fact, we even had a team of four braver-than-average gals, equipped with steel-rimmed brooms, we had dubbed "The Rat Patrol" for our floor. This fearless foursome was often called to pounce upon and eradicate some tiny, grey-brown furball.

It was "quiet hour" in the dorm. I was studying in my corner room and dutifully patrolling the hall periodically to encourage other students to do the same when the stillness was suddenly split by Pam's scream. I ran down the hall and cautiously opened Pam's door with my master key. There was Pam dancing around on top of the desk and her roommate Cynthia bouncing up and down in the middle of the bed.

"It's a rat! It's a rat!" they screamed.

Quickly I called for The Rat Patrol who appeared as Wonder Women from nowhere with their rat ridders. We hustled Pam and Cynthia out of the room and closed the door to try and trap the little monster. We searched diligently, but to no avail. The mouse had escaped through some secret varmint passageway unknown to humans.

However, I knew there would be no rest on our floor unless we produced evidence that the vicious monster had been defeated. So, we plotted.

At the signal, I yelled, "There he goes! Get 'im!" We slammed our brooms against the floor, moved furniture around, and made a general hullabaloo for a couple of minutes. At last we let out a victory cry, "We got him!" Then I took an empty Dippity Doo jar out of the trash and dropped it into a used Mac Eplan's pink cookie bag and held the top tightly in my hand as we walked triumphantly out of the room past Pam and Cynthia.

"Well, girls," I said, "you don't have to worry about that mouse anymore." Then I shook the sack to make the jar thud on the bottom as if it were the deceased mouse.

We all slept very well that night. And that just goes to show you that it's not the *actual* truth but what you *believe* to be the truth that governs your actions.

I've often pondered since then about how many rats there are in my own life that I have chosen to believe have been eradicated. I may chase them around in my mind occasionally, but they escape through a rathole in my id to terrorize me another day. And, perhaps, I've fallen peacefully asleep thinking the danger is gone when it may actually be lurking beneath my mental bed. I wonder.... Maybe I'll give that some serious thought tomorrow.

Ho hum and good night.

The Old Refrain

F ritz Kreisler, the violinist, found himself in Hamburg one evening with an hour to spare before taking his boat to London where he was to play the following evening. So, he wandered into a music shop.

The proprietor asked to see his violin which he carried under his arm. In a moment he disappeared, to reappear with two policemen. One laid his hand on Kreisler's shoulder and said, "You are under arrest."

"For what?" asked Kreisler.

"You have Fritz Kreisler's violin."

"Well, I am Fritz Kreisler."

"Come, come," said the policeman, "you cannot pull that one on us. Come to the station."

Kreisler's boat sailed in an hour. He had to do some quick thinking.

He looked around and in the corner saw a Victrola. Kreisler asked the proprietor if he had any of Fritz Kreisler's records. He produced *The Old Refrain*, put it on and played it through.

"Now," Kreisler said, "let me have my violin." Then, with whatever skill he could command he played *The Old Refrain*. When Kreisler was through, he asked, "Are you satisfied now?"

With profuse apologies, they bowed him out to freedom.

Sometimes when one of life's hallelujahs is in our very presence, we don't recognize it. Perhaps, we have grown a bit farsighted in our living. We look *out there* for happiness, when all the time happiness is *in here*. Searching for hallelujahs begins in your own heart.

*When words
leave off,
music begins.*

—HEINRICH HEINE

Without music,
life would be
a mistake.

—UNKNOWN

I Wish You Love

I wish you the courage to be warm when the world would prefer that you be cool.

I wish you success sufficient to your needs; I wish you failure to temper that success.

I wish you joy in all your days; I wish you sadness so that you may better measure joy.

I wish you gladness to overbalance grief.

I wish you humor and a twinkle in the eye.

I wish you glory and the strength to bear its burdens.

I wish you sunshine on your path and storms to season your journey.

I wish you peace—in the world in

which you live and in the smallest corner of the heart where truth is kept.

I wish you faith—to help define your living and your life.

More I cannot wish you—except perhaps love—to make all the rest worthwhile.

—ROBERT A. WARD

..and in conclusion

t was Sunday morning, and my friend James was wrapping up his sermon of the day. He'd done an excellent job with his topic, he was thinking to himself, when the disruption occurred.

One of the older men in the church had been sitting about halfway back. He and his wife were parents of a tiny, two-year-old surprise package that had been delivered to them late in life. The wife was out of town for a day or two, and the man had spent the entire sermon trying to keep that little bundle of energy under reverent control.

Finally, just as James was ready to make his concluding point, the man could take no more. So, he picked up the little girl and started out the back of the auditorium to apply some good old homemade discipline to the appropriate place. Walking out, he had his back to James, but the tot, being carried in typical over-the-shoulder fashion, was facing James.

Now, little Betsy was familiar with this exit routine and fully aware of its coming reward. So, just as the father pushed through the double swinging doors out of the auditorium, she threw out her arms to James and screamed in a plaintive wail, "Save me!"

James later confessed that the rest of his sermon was strictly anticlimactic.

We could all take a lesson from Betsy, though. When you're up to your ears in trouble in this life, and it looks as if the worst is yet to come, don't be afraid to throw out your arms to God and call for help. He'll hear you, and he'll answer.

Hallelujah! and Amen.